"DO YOU KNOW"

It's an introductory handbook with some amazing animals and their interesting facts.

EDITED BY

SANJOY MAHATA

This book is an assembled knowledge bank for the beginners to the Animal World. Some amazing animals with their interesting facts have been presented for kids. This book will attract the kids to learn about the Animal World.

All the information has been collected from The Internet and various knowledge encyclopaedias'. So, no copyright will be applicable for any content of this book. Copyright will be applicable only on the book's design, decoration and presentation style.

First Edition: 24th September, 2020

ISBN No: 978-93-5416-349-4

No. of Pages : 43

"DO YOU KNOW"

Table of content

1

I am the Beautiful bird from India.

Some of my relatives live in different parts of Asia, Africa and Australia.

Come to visit me in the monsoon. I will show you my dance with beautiful feathers.

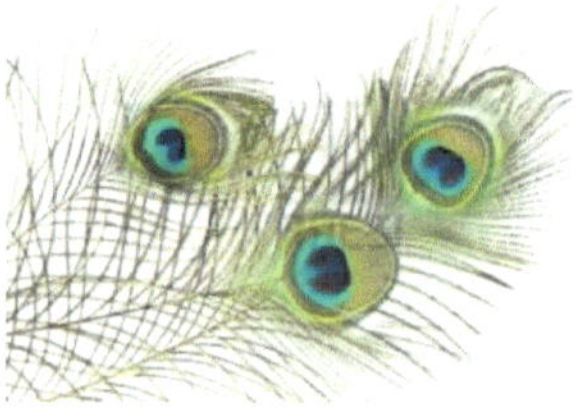

"I AM A "PEACOCK". MY WIFE NAMED AS "PEAHEN". OUR BABIES ARE CALLED AS "PEACHICKS""

Peacocks are large, colourful pheasants (typically blue and green) known for their iridescent tails. These tail feathers, or coverts, spread out in a distinctive train that is more than 60 percent of the bird's total body length and boast colourful "eye" markings of blue, gold, red, and other hues.

Order: Galliformes
Class: Aves
Kingdom: Animalia
Family: Phasianidae

2

"I AM A RAT. ACCORDING TO THE AUSTRALIAN BROADCASTING CORP., OUR MALES ARE CALLED BUCKS; FEMALES ARE DOES. INFANTS ARE CALLED PUPS OR KITTENS"

Rats are various medium-sized, long-tailed rodents. Species of rats are found throughout the order Rodentia, but stereotypical rats are found in the genus Rattus. Other rat genera include Neotoma (pack rats), Bandicota (bandicoot rats) and Dipodomys (kangaroo rats).

Kingdom: Animalia
Phylum: Chordata
Class: Mammalia
Order: Rodentia

3

I am the little danger of South American rivers and lakes.

My Brazilian relatives may be dangerous for you too.

"WE ARE NEITHER CARNIVOROUS NOR AGGRESSIVE MAN-EATERS. IN FACT, IF WE HAVE EATEN ANY HUMANS IT'S MORE LIKELY BECAUSE THEY HAVE EATEN THE REMAINS OF A CORPSE LYING ON THE RIVER BED."

Piranhas are South American fish with razor-sharp teeth and a reputation for feeding frenzies. In fact, piranha means "tooth fish" in the Brazilian language of the Tupi people. ... Two species, Pygocentrus and Serrasalmus, are popular as aquarium fish

Family: Serrasalmidae　　**Class**: Actinopterygii
Kingdom: Animalia　　**Phylum**: Chordata

4

Don't laugh at me.

I have a surprising feature.

Yes! I can fly. Aahh! I am nor a bird.

"I AM WALLACE'S FLYING FROGS. THE MEMBRANES BETWEEN MY TOES AND LOOSE SKIN FLAPS ON AND CATCHES THE AIR, HELPING ME TO GLIDE. I CAN FLY 50 FEET OR MORE."

Wallace's flying frogs are not the only frogs who have developed this ability, but they are among the largest. The black color of their foot webbing helps distinguish them from their similarly aerial cousins. They are generally bright green with yellow sides and grow to about 4 inches. They survive mainly on insects.

Species: R. Nigropalmatus
Kingdom: Animalia
Order: Anura
Genus: Rhacophorus

5

"I, THE KANGAROO RAT OF NORTH AMERICA AM ONE OF THE MOST SPECIALIZED ANIMALS LIVING IN THE DESERT ENVIRONMENTS AND CAN GO FOR MY ENTIRE LIFE WITHOUT WATER."

Kangaroo rats are four-toed heteromyid rodents with big hind legs, small front legs and relatively large heads. Adults typically weigh between 70 and 170 grams (2.5 and 6.0 oz). The tails of kangaroo rats are longer than both their bodies and their heads.

Genus: Dipodomys
Kingdom: Animalia
Phylum: Chordata
Order: Rodentia

6

Hi!

I am the tiniest monkey.

I am lighter than an apple.

Come to me to enjoy the fun on the top of AMAZON.

"WE, THE PYGMY MARMOSETS ARE THE FUNNY ANIMALS THAT CAN FIT INTO HUMAN PALM. OUR FEMALES ARE SLIGHTLY LARGER THAN MALES. ON AVERAGE, WE REACH BETWEEN 4.75 AND 6 INCHES IN LENGTH AND WEIGHT BETWEEN 3.53 AND 4 OUNCES."

The pygmy marmoset is a small monkey native to rainforests of the western Amazon Basin in South America. It is notable for being the smallest monkey and one of the smallest primates in the world.

Genus: Cebuella
Order: Primates
Kingdom: Animalia
Phylum: Chordata

7

I am able to literally slip with one eye open.
I can also communicate with my little children while they are still in the eggs.
Surprised! Ha Ha!

“THE TERM "GOOSE" IS MORE PROPERLY USED FOR FEMALE BIRD, WHILE "GANDER" REFERS SPECIFICALLY TO A MALE ONE. THE YOUNG BIRDS BEFORE FLEDGING ARE CALLED GOSLINGS.”

A goose is a bird of any of several waterfowl species in the family Anatidae. This group comprises the genera Anser, Branta, and Chen, the latter sometimes being placed within the genus Anser. Some other birds, mostly related to the shelducks, have "goose" as part of their names.

8

THE LARGEST NEST ON RECORD WAS MADE BY A PAIR OF BALD EAGLES. IT WAS 2.9 METRES (9.5 FT) IN DIAMETER, 6 METRES (20 FT) DEEP AND WAS ESTIMATED TO WEIGH MORE THAN 2 TONNES (4,400 LB).

The bald eagle is a bird of prey found in North America. A sea eagle, it has two known subspecies and forms a species pair with the white-tailed eagle. Its range includes most of Canada and Alaska, all of the contiguous United States, and northern Mexico.

Species: H. Leucocephalus
Genus: Haliaeetus
Kingdom: Animalia
Phylum: Chordata

9

I am the largest bird in the World.

I have three stomachs.

I cannot fly, but I can run fast.

OSTRICHES ARE THE FAST RUNNERS OF ANY BIRDS OR OTHER TWO-LEGGED ANIMAL AND CAN SPRINT AT OVER 70 KM/HR, COVERING UP TO 5M IN A SINGLE STRIDE.

The flightless ostrich is the world's largest bird. Today ostriches are only found natively in the wild in Africa, where they occur in a range of open arid and semi-arid habitats such as savannas and the Sahel

Family: Struthionidae Order: Struthioniformes
Genus: Struthio Class: Aves

10

I am a cute bird.

I can reach your friend to give your letter.

I am proud as my grand relatives had participated on World War I & II.

THE ROCK PIGEON WAS USED IN BOTH WORLD WAR I AND II, NOTABLY BY THE AUSTRALIAN, FRENCH, GERMAN, AMERICAN, AND UK FORCES.

The rock dove, rock pigeon, or common pigeon; Columba livia is a member of the bird family Columbidae (doves and pigeons). In common usage, this bird is often simply referred to as the "pigeon".

Species: C. Livia
Genus: Columba
Kingdom: Animalia
Order: Columbiformes

11

Hi!

I am the cute being from China.

I have no more jobs without eating and sleeping.

I can climb on tree and also swim in water.

A 45-KILO ADULT (AND PANDAS CAN REACH 150 KG IN CAPTIVITY) SPENDS AS LONG AS 14 HOURS EATING. AND IT CAN EAT 12 TO 38 KILOS OF BAMBOO A DAY.

The giant panda also known as the panda bear or simply the panda is a bear native to south central China. It is characterized by large, black patches around it's...

Species: A. Melanoleuca
Genus: Ailuropoda
Phylum: Chordata
Kingdom: Animalia

12

I am the cute loving bird.

I can talk on your language if you train me.

Ahha! I love chilli. Do you?

PARROTS ARE FOUND IN WARM CLIMATES ALL OVER MOST OF THE WORLD. THE GREATEST DIVERSITIES EXIST IN AUSTRALASIA, CENTRAL AMERICA, AND SOUTH AMERICA.

Parrots have curved bills (beaks), strong legs and clawed feet. Parrots are often brightly coloured. Parrots are believed to be one of the most intelligent bird species. Some species are known for imitating human voices.

Phylum: Chordata
Kingdom: Animalia
Clade: Psittacopasserae
Order: Psittaciformes

13

LARGE PENGUIN POPULATIONS CAN BE FOUND IN COUNTRIES SUCH AS NEW ZEALAND, AUSTRALIA, CHILE, ARGENTINA AND SOUTH AFRICA. NO PENGUINS LIVE AT THE NORTH POLE. PENGUINS EAT A RANGE OF FISH AND OTHER SEA LIFE THAT THEY CATCH UNDERWATER.

Almost all penguin species are native to the Southern Hemisphere. They are not found in North Hemisphere.
Penguins can drink sea water.
Penguins spend around half their time in water and the other half on land.

Family: Spheniscidae
Class: Aves
Kingdom: Animalia
Phylum: Chordata

14

Hi Kids!

I am a small cute looking bird.

Do you love me?

I will catch fish for you from river.

A KINGFISHER, SAID TO BE THE FIRST BIRD TO FLY FROM NOAH'S ARK AFTER THE DELUGE, SUPPOSEDLY RECEIVED THE ORANGE OF THE SETTING SUN ON ITS BREAST AND THE BLUE OF THE SKY ON ITS BACK.

Kingfishers are a family of small to medium-sized, brightly coloured birds in the order Coraciiformes. They have a cosmopolitan distribution, with most species found in the tropical regions of Africa, Asia, and Oceania.

Family: Alcedinida
Order: Coraciiformes
Kingdom: Animalia
Class: Aves

15

I am a powerful flyer bird.

I can fly over the Himalayas.

I can also stand on one leg for hours.

THROUGHOUT ASIA,
THE CRANE IS A SYMBOL OF HAPPINESS AND ETERNAL YOUTH. IN JAPAN, THE CRANE IS ONE OF THE MYSTICAL OR HOLY CREATURES
AND SYMBOLIZES GOOD FORTUNE AND LONGEVITY.

Cranes live on all continents except Antarctica and South America. They are opportunistic feeders that change their diets according to the season and their own nutrient requirements. They eat a range of items from suitably sized small rodents, fish, amphibians, and insects to grain and berries.

Species: G. Grus
Genus: Grus
Family: Gruidae
Class: Aves

16

"Cheer-up,
cheerily, cheer-up,
cheer-up,
cheerily."
- Do you hear me?

You must love me
to you listen my
"TRUE ROBIN

ONLY THE MALE ROBIN SINGS THE "TRUE ROBIN SONG," AND HE SINGS IT TO DECLARE HIS PERSONAL NESTING TERRITORY. THE ROBIN WAS DECLARED BRITAIN'S NATIONAL BIRD ON DECEMBER 15TH, 1960.

The European robin (Erithacus rubecula), known simply as the robin or robin redbreast in the ... In the 15th century, when it became popular to give human names to familiar species, the bird came to be known as robin redbreast

Species: E. rubecula
Genus: Erithacus
Kingdom: Animalia
Phylum: Chordata

17

CATS CAN ROTATE THEIR EARS 180 DEGREES.

CATS SPEND 70% OF THEIR LIVES SLEEPING.

A CAT WAS THE MAYOR OF AN ALASKAN TOWN FOR 20 YEARS.

The cat (Felis catus) is a domestic species of small carnivorous mammal. It is the only domesticated species in the family Felidae and is often referred to as the domestic cat to distinguish it from the wild members of the family.

Species: F. Catus
Genus: Felis
Phylum: Chordata
Kingdom: Animalia

18

I am the smallest bird. I can fly forward, backward and even upside down. I can't walk or run.

HUMMINGBIRDS HAVE THE LARGEST BRAINS OF THE WILD BIRD GROUP. ONLY HUMMINGBIRDS CAN FLY UP, DOWN, SIDEWAYS, FORWARDS, AND, BACKWARDS!

Hummingbirds are the second largest family of birds with over 300 species. Hummingbirds have weak feet – they mainly use them just for perching. Hummingbirds are found only in the Western Hemisphere, with almost half the species living in the "equatorial belt" between 10 degrees north and south of the equator.

Family: Trochilidae
Order: Apodiformes
Class: Aves
Kingdom: Animalia

19

Hey!

I am the big boss of Jungle.

Always keep safe distance from me.

My one punch may kill you.

TIGERS ARE THE LARGEST AMONGST OTHER WILD CATS.

TIGER CUBS ARE BORN BLIND AND ONLY HALF OF THE CUBS SURVIVE.

TIGERS LOVE TO SWIM AND PLAY IN THE WATER.

The tiger is the largest extant cat species and a member of the genus Panthera. It is most recognizable for its dark vertical stripes on orange-brown fur with a lighter underside. It is an apex predator, primarily preying on ungulates such as deer and wild boar.

Species: P. Tigris
Kingdom: Animalia
Phylum: Chordata
Genus: Panthera

20

Hey!
I am waiting for you in Malaysia.

I have build in crampon on my head.

I am the symbol of Malaysian Democratic Action Party.

HORNBILLS NEST IN THE HOLES OF HOLLOW TREES. THE FEMALE SEALS THE HOLE WITH CLAY AND FAECES, LEAVING ONLY A SMALL HOLE IN THE WALL TO RECEIVE FOOD FROM HER MATE.

The hornbills (Bucerotidae) are a family of bird found in tropical and subtropical Africa, Asia and Melanesia. They are characterized by a long, down-curved bill which is frequently brightly colored and sometimes has a casque on the upper mandible.

Species: B. bicornis
Family: Bucerotidae
Class: Aves
Kingdom: Animalia

21

"When weather gets cool;
Come to me and get wool"

- Ha Ha ! You know me from your 1st rhyme book.

Our relatives are mentioned repeatedly in the Bible too.

SHEEP ARE KNOWN TO SELF-MEDICATE WHEN THEY HAVE SOME ILLNESSES. THEY WILL EAT SPECIFIC PLANTS WHEN ILL THAT CAN CURE THEM. SHEEP HAVE AN EXCELLENT MEMORY. THEY CAN REMEMBER INDIVIDUAL SHEEP AND HUMANS FOR YEARS.

Sheep, species of domesticated ruminant mammal, raised for its meat, milk, and wool. The sheep is usually stockier than its relative the goat; its horns, when present, are more divergent.

Species: O. aries
Genus: Ovis
Phylum: Chordata
Order: Artiodactyla

22

Hello!
I am the national icon of New Zealand.
I have no tail but I have whiskers, like a Cat.

KIWI HAS TINY WINGS, BUT CANNOT FLY. IT IS THE ONLY BIRD IN THE WORLD WITH NOSTRILS AT THE END OF ITS BEAK. IT HAS NO TAIL FEATHERS, BUT DOES HAVE WHISKERS, LIKE A CAT.

The kiwi is a unique and curious bird: it cannot fly, has loose, hair-like feathers, strong legs and no tail. Learn more about the kiwi, the national icon of New Zealand and unofficial national emblem. New Zealanders have been called 'Kiwis' since the nickname was bestowed by Australian soldiers in the First World War.

Genus: Apteryx
Family: Apterygidae
Phylum: Chordata
Kingdom: Animalia

23

KANGAROOS GENERALLY LIVE IN SMALL GROUPS CALLED 'MOBS' WITH AROUND 10 FEMALES AND THEIR JOEYS AND ONE OR TWO MALES. IN AREAS WITH LOTS OF FOOD THOUGH, HUGE GATHERINGS OF AROUND 1500 KANGAROOS HAVE BEEN OBSERVED.

The kangaroo is a marsupial from the family Macropodidae (macropods, meaning "large foot"). In common use the term is used to describe the largest species from this family, the red kangaroo, as well as the antilopine kangaroo, eastern grey kangaroo, and western grey kangaroo.

Order: Diprotodontia   Family: Macropodidae
Class: Mammalia   Kingdom: Animalia

24

I am the largest flying bird.
I have the longest wingspan too.
We range widely in the South Ocean
and the North Pacific.

ALBATROSSES LIVE TOGETHER, AND THEY USUALLY NEST ON ISLANDS WHERE NO PEOPLE LIVE. MANY BULLER'S ALBATROSSES AND BLACK-FOOTED ALBATROSSES NEST UNDER TREES IN OPEN FOREST.

Great Albatrosses are among the largest of flying birds. All albatrosses are very good at flying, spending much of their life in the air. They eat squid, fish and krill.

Albatrosses are masters of soaring flight, able to glide over vast tracts of ocean without flapping their wings.

Class: Aves Order: Procellariiformes
Family: Diomedeidae

25

Hey!

I am the Camel's hippie cousin.

I am the smart.

I make excellent guard for herbs of small animals.

LLAMAS LIVE ALL OVER THE PLANET – IN AUSTRALIA, EUROPE AND NORTH AMERICA, ON THE SOUTH AMERICAN CONTINENT. THEY ARE PARTICULARLY PREVALENT IN PERU.

The llama is a domesticated South American camelid, widely used as a meat and pack animal by Andean cultures since the Pre-Columbian era. Llamas are very social animals and live with others as a herd. Their wool is very soft and lanolin-free. Llamas can learn simple tasks after a few repetitions.

Genus: Lama
Family: Camelidae
Order: Artiodactyla
Class: Mammalia

26

Hi!

I am a fish who can survive out of water.

I am famous for my ability to walk.

I can climb on a tree too.

ANABAS IS ABLE TO SURVIVE FOR SEVERAL DAYS OR WEEKS OUT OF WATER IF THE AIR BREATHING ORGANS CAN BE KEPT MOIST.

Anabas, the climbing perch, is a species of fish in the family Anabantidae, the climbing gouramis. It is native to Asia, where it occurs from India east to China and to the Wallace Line. It is an invasive species that can live without water for 6-10 hours.

Anabas is quite famous for its ability to walk; important food fish in SE Asia considered as a tasty food fish but not of the finest quality since it is bony

Species: A. testudineus   Family: Anabantidae

Order: Anabantiformes   Class: Actinopterygii

27

Hello!
I am a cute sea bird.
My beak changes colour during the year.
I can hold several fishes in my bill at a time.

THE ATLANTIC PUFFIN HAS BECOME ICELAND'S MOST PRECIOUS BIRD AND A TOURIST ATTRACTION. HE IS BOTH CAPTIVATING AND PECULIAR AND HAS BEEN NICKNAMED 'SEA PARROT', 'PENGUIN OF THE NORTH' AND EVEN 'CLOWN OF THE SEA' AND IS ALSO KNOWN AS THE COMMON PUFFIN. IN ICELAND WE JUST CALL HIM 'LUNDI'.

The Atlantic puffin has black and white feathers and a large and colourful beak. It is a seabird in the auk family that breeds in and around Iceland. Puffins can be seen in Iceland from early April until late August.

Species: F. arctica
Genus: Fratercula
Family: Alcidae
Phylum: Chordata

28

Hey! Meet me.

I am the power king of JUNGLE.

I am the largest land mammal of the World.

There is a saying - "We never forget".

ELEPHANT TUSKS ARE ACTUALLY ENLARGED TEETH WHICH FIRST APPEAR WHEN ELEPHANTS ARE AROUND 2 YEARS OLD. TUSKS CONTINUE GROWING THROUGHOUT THEIR LIVES.

Elephants are mammals of the family Elephantidae and the largest existing land animals. Three species are currently recognized: the African bush elephant, the African forest elephant, and the Asian elephant.

Elephants calves are able to stand within 20 minutes of being born and can walk within 1 hour.

Family: Elephantidae **Order**: Proboscidea
Kingdom: Animalia **Class**: Mammalia

29

THE MUSCLES THAT OPEN CROCODILES JAWS HOWEVER ARE NOT SO POWERFUL, REASONABLY STRONG PEOPLE COULD HOLD A CROCODILES JAW CLOSED WITH THEIR BARE HANDS.

Crocodiles are large semi aquatic reptiles that live throughout the tropics in Africa, Asia, the Americas and Australia.

Although Crocodile can't die of natural aging, they also can't live forever. Nature has a way of killing them. The way they die is out of starvation or if they contract a disease. They keep growing throughout their lifespan and they require more and more food.

Kingdom: Animalia
Phylum: Chordata
Family: Crocodylidae
Class: Reptilia

30

Hey!

I am Frigatebird.

I can spend entire week in the air.

FRIGATE BIRDS HAVE LONG WINGS, TAILS AND BILLS AND THE MALES HAVE A RED POUCH THAT IS INFLATED DURING THE BREEDING SEASON TO ATTRACT A MATE.

FEMALES ARE BLACK BUT HAVE A WHITE BREAST AND LOWER NECK SIDES, A BROWN BAND ON THE WINGS AND A BLUE EYE-RING.

Frigate birds are a family of seabirds called Fregatidae which are found across all tropical and subtropical oceans. The five extant species are classified in a single genus, Fregata. All have predominantly black plumage, long, deeply forked tails and long hooked bills.

Genus: Fregata	Kingdom: Animalia
Order: Suliformes	Class: Aves

31

ALL OF THEM HAVE RATTLES, ARE VENOMOUS AND ARE PIT VIPERS. RATTLESNAKES FEED ON RODENTS, SQUIRRELS, RABBITS AND OTHER SMALL CRITTERS. RATTLESNAKE EGGS WILL STAY INSIDE THEIR MOTHER UNTIL THEY HATCH.

Rattlesnakes range in size depending on the species from one to eight feet in length. They are usually thick bodied snakes and come in a variety of colors and patterns. Most species have some sort of dark diamond shaped patterns on their skin against a lighter colored background. They also have a triangular head.

Family: Viperidae
Class: Reptilia
Kingdom: Animalia
Order: Squamata

32

Hey!

Look at me.

My special tails are different from other birds.

THE RIBBON-TAILED ASTRAPIA IS DISTRIBUTED AND ENDEMIC TO SUBALPINE FORESTS IN WESTERN PART OF THE CENTRAL HIGHLANDS OF PAPUA NEW GUINEA.

Another bird with a unique tail, the male ribbon-tailed astrapia boasts white ribbon-like tails that can grow up to 1 metre in length! The tails contrast their sleek black bodies, and with their mesmerizing iridescent heads, they're really an unusual sight to see. Their extremely long tails can get in the way sometimes, so they have to spend time untangling them before flight – definitely not a survival advantage, but it helps them attract the females.

Phylum: Chordata
Order: Passerine
Species: A. mayeri
Class: Aves

33

OKAPI MOTHERS PRODUCE INFRASONIC CALLS AT AROUND 14HZ TO COMMUNICATE WITH THEIR CALVES, WHICH ARE USEFUL IN DENSE FOREST AND CANNOT BE HEARD BY HUMANS.

The Okapi, also known as the forest giraffe, Congolese giraffe, or zebra giraffe, is an artiodactyl mammal native to the northeast of the Democratic Republic of the Congo in Central Africa. Although the okapi has striped markings reminiscent of zebras, it is most closely related to the giraffe.

Species: O. johnstoni
Genus: Okapia
Kingdom: Animalia
Phylum: Chordata

34

ALL CLOWNFISH ARE BORN MALE. WHEN THE DOMINANT FEMALE DIES, THE DOMINANT MALE WILL TURN ITSELF INTO A FEMALE.

CLOWNFISH COMMUNICATE BY MAKING POPPING AND CLICKING NOISES.

Clownfish live in the warm waters of sheltered reefs and shallow seas in the Pacific and Indian Oceans. During the winter, they will migrate to deeper water to stay warm.

Clownfish are omnivores. They eat dead anemone tentacles, leftovers from the anemone, plankton, mollusk, zooplankton, phytoplankton, small crustaceans and various algae.

Phylum: Chordata　　Class: Actinopterygii

Family: Pomacentridae　　Kingdom: Animalia

35

Hey!!

I am the loudest animal in the New World.

I am also the largest monkey in the Latin American Rainforests.

UNLIKE OLD WORLD MONKEYS, HOWLERS AND OTHER NEW WORLD SPECIES HAVE A PREHENSILE TAIL. THEY CAN USE THIS TAIL AS AN EXTRA ARM TO GRIP OR EVEN HANG FROM BRANCHES.

Howler monkeys are among the largest of the New World monkeys. They are famous for their loud howls, which can travel 5 km through dense rain forest. These monkeys are native to South and Central American forests.

Genus: Alouatta
Family: Atelidae

Kingdom: Animalia
Phylum: Chordata

36

IT IS ACTUALLY THE MALE THAT HAS THE BRIGHT PLUMAGE. THE FEMALE HAS BROWN FEATHERS. THIS DIFFERENCE IN APPEARANCE BETWEEN THE GENDERS IS KNOWN AS 'SEXUAL DIMORPHISM'.

Cock-of-the-rock is found in tropical and subtropical rainforests close to rocky areas, where they build their nests. The genus is composed of only two known extant species: the Andean cock-of-the-rock and the smaller Guianan cock-of-the-rock.

Species: R. peruvianus Genus: Rupicola
Family: Cotingidae Order: Passeriformes

37

I am the largest Rodent.

I am a fantastic swimmer.

I can even sleep in the water too.

CAPYBARAS OFTEN REFERRED TO AS "MOVING CHAIRS", THESE FRIENDLY CRITTERS DON'T EVER SEEM TO KNOCK BACK A RIDE SHARING REQUEST FROM ANOTHER ANIMAL. A WHOLE HOST OF BIRD SPECIES, MONKEYS, RABBITS, AND EVEN OTHER CAPYBARAS HAVE BEEN SPOTTED SEATED, PERCHED OR LAYING ON THE BACK OF A MUCH-OBLIGING CAPYBARA.

The capybara is a giant cavy rodent native to South America. It is the largest living rodent in the world. Also called capivara, chigüire, chigüiro, carpincho and ronsoco, it is a member of the genus Hydrochoerus, of which the only other extant member is the lesser capybara.

Phylum: Chordata
Species: H. hydrochaeris
Class: Mammalia
Kingdom: Animalia

38

THE KING COBRA BUILDS A NEST. FIRST, THE FEMALE GATHERS LEAVES, USING HER COILS AS A MAKESHIFT RAKE. AFTER SHE LAYS 20 TO 30 EGGS IN THE MIDDLE, SHE GATHERS MORE LEAVES; LAYERING THEM OVER HER CLUTCH.

The king cobra, also known as the hamadryad, is a venomous snake species in the family Elapidae, endemic to forests from India through Southeast Asia. It is threatened by habitat destruction and has been listed as Vulnerable on the IUCN Red List since 2010. It is the world's longest venomous snake.

Phylum: Chordata
Kingdom: Animalia
Species: O. Hannah
Genus: Ophiophagus

39

IT HAS BEEN PROVED BY SCIENTISTS THAT DOLPHINS GIVE THEMSELVES NAMES. THEY DEVELOP THEIR OWN INDIVIDUAL WHISTLES AND THEY RECOGNIZE THEIRS AND OTHER DOLPHINS' NAMES.

WHEN THEY ARE ASLEEP, ONE PART OF THEIR BRAIN REMAINS ALERT AND AWAKE.

Dolphin is a common name of aquatic mammals within the infraorder Cetacea. The term dolphin usually refers to the extant families Delphinidae, Platanistidae, Iniidae, and Pontoporiidae, and the extinct Lipotidae. There are 40 extant species named as dolphins.

Order: Artiodactyla
Class: Mammalia
Kingdom: Animalia
Infraorder: Cetacea

www.ingramcontent.com/pod-product-compliance
Ingram Content Group UK Ltd.
Pitfield, Milton Keynes, MK11 3LW, UK
UKHW061433190726
13845UKWH00020B/163
9789354163494